A Dark Dreambox of Another Kind
The Poems of **Alfred Starr Hamilton**

Edited by Ben Estes and Alan Felsenthal

Introduction by Geof Hewitt

The Song Cave

Published by The Song Cave
www.the-song-cave.com
© 2013 Virginia G. Cruickshank
Foreword © 2013 Ben Estes and Alan Felsenthal
Introduction © 2013 Geof Hewitt
Cover photograph © 1967 Simpson Kalisher
Design and layout by Mary Austin Speaker

ISBN 978-0-9884643-0-8
Library of Congress cataloging-in-publication data has been applied for.

SECOND PRINTING

Table of Contents

———

Final Notebooks

Foreword

Allow the soul back into poetry. Admit that there is a house on top of the moon. And exploring that house makes living in one on earth more bearable. This is the house of speaking in nursery rhymes, the place a poet goes to look at stars. Find a way to rebel against the establishment (even the Poetry establishment). Do not follow a good man; follow his work. Find his work in these pages—Alfred Starr Hamilton's *Dark Dreambox of Another Kind*.

Few know what to do with a mystic poet these days. When one shows up, we are taught that there are "timelier visions," other ways of living through poetry. Terms such as *outsider, untrained,* and *peripheral* have all been applied to the poetry of Alfred Starr Hamilton. In introducing his work to a new generation of readers, we hesitate to apply these labels exclusively, for fear that their connotations may hinder readers from perceiving his poems as fully and consciously constructed—the real thing. Hamilton was a poet through and through, who wrote openly and all the time. At various points in his life he wanted very much to be published. Unfortunately, although some literary magazines did feature his writing, he never found much of an audience. He did not teach or give public readings to promote his work. He stayed out of both mainstream and literary society in the 1960s, '70s, and '80s. He inhabited his own consciousness as though divine, insisted that poetry had chosen him, and lived in a realm of spiritual privilege that "professional" poets are usually barred from.

Alfred Starr Hamilton was born on June 14, 1914 (Flag Day), to a well-established East Coast family that, along with many other such families, lost much of its money during the Great Depression. However, the family kept its large home on Clinton Avenue in Montclair, New Jersey, where Alfred grew up with his mother and father, his two older sisters, and, later on, his sister Judith's children. Alfred took great care of his older sister Katherine who had cerebral palsy.

Alfred's eldest niece, Jane Huber, whose papers and interviews provide the basis for most of our biographical knowledge of Alfred, remembers "the day by day evolving of his fear of the wind, his fear of bees, and his dislike of string beans." Alfred's niece Virginia Cruickshank, who grew up in the family home with Alfred years later, remembers the adult Hamilton as a solitary man who was relatively quiet, spending his days sitting at the typewriter in his upstairs bedroom. He once had a black cat named Anonymous.

During World War II Hamilton ended up getting stationed on the West Coast, was quickly discharged, and returned east to his family home. The details surrounding the discharge, along with many other details of his personal history, are still quite unclear. He claimed that he'd gone A.W.O.L. after realizing he couldn't stand the regimentation of military life; yet when he died in 2005 he was buried with honors in a military cemetery. He wanted his gravestone to read "A.W.O.L." The story Hamilton told of his dishonorable discharge may have been a manifestation of his psychological troubles, which also marked his heartbreaking letters to the various editors and publishers of his poems and the local Montclair police department.

Besides this short stint in the military, Hamilton only held a couple of jobs during his lifetime. First, as a Fuller Brush salesman during the 1930s, when he was significantly less shy and solitary than in his later years; and later, filling gumball machines housed in the shops around Montclair. He stored these machines in the basement of the family home until the morning that he came upstairs and announced to his family that he just "couldn't look at them anymore." After his mother's death, Alfred lived on a small inheritance of $1,000 a year. Barely making ends meet, he rented an $80-a-month room on the ground floor of a rooming house on South Willow Street ("The Walden House"), just down the street from the home he grew up in. It was during his residence there that the bulk of the poems in this edition were written.

In the early 1960s, after taking a brief trip to Ithaca with his family, Hamilton fatefully decided to submit poems to Cornell University's literary magazine *Epoch*. He sent roughly 45 poems each week to their office, which was unable to handle this quantity of work. Eventually, under the leadership of David Ray and the editorial assistance of Geof Hewitt, a number of Hamilton's poems were published—which only encouraged Hamilton to send more. Apparently, there were boxes filled with Hamilton's poems sitting around the offices and in the homes of *Epoch*'s editors for decades.

Eventually, Hewitt found a home for Hamilton's work at Jonathan Williams' famed Jargon Society, which published *The Poems of Alfred Starr Hamilton* in 1970. Until now, it is the only full-length collection of his work ever to be published. Despite the efforts of editors of a dozen or so small journals across the country during the 1970s and '80s, Hamilton's work has never had more than a small cult following. The two chapbooks published during his lifetime, *Sphinx* and *The Big Parade*, had small print runs, and the Jargon Society book did not sell enough copies to warrant a second printing.

The last few years of Hamilton's life were spent in a nursing home where, according to the nurses, he was fairly uncommunicative. Having heard that he liked to write poems, they offered him some notebooks and pencils, and eventually he began writing in them. After his death, Alfred's niece contacted the nursing home to retrieve his personal belongings and was told that the janitor had saved some remaining items from Hamilton's bedside table in a large manila envelope. Along with some scraps of paper and receipts were a few notebooks containing his last poems. These poems continue Hamilton's reflective poetry, and document Hamilton's confrontation with old age, love, death, and the afterlife. The poems were written in a very shaky hand; we've done our best in transcribing a selection and are happy to be able to offer many of them in this volume.

Aside from the notebooks found after his death, the only surviving poems written by Hamilton are the poems that found their way into publication during his lifetime, and the poems that Jonathan Williams edited out of the Jargon Society book (most of which we have included here in ours). Of all the thousands of poems he was known to have written, each was typed up a single time—with no duplicate. Thousands of poems have been lost to time. In the absence of a clear chronology, for this volume we've decided to present the poems as we ourselves would want to approach them as readers: grouped in ways that we hope will allow readers to trace the motifs throughout his work.

If you have encountered the wonderland of Hamilton's writings before, we are happy to welcome you back. If this is your first time, prepare to enter a house of metaphor, where life is a poem and in it there is always more to be discovered. Hamilton's is an extremely gentle language cultured in loneliness, the product of encountering a world while staying away from it. His poetry is miraculous in its humility, inviting as ever, and filled with warmth and concern for its readers.

Ben Estes and Alan Felsenthal

Introduction

Great art transforms how we see things. Interesting how *see* implies the visual and graphic arts when a more accurate verb would be *perceive*. Inventors create new ways. e. e. cummings showed a new way to perceive poetry, creating great art not only in itself, but in its influence. Savvy poets might want to study how e. e. found his market, or how the market found e. e.

Alfred Starr Hamilton didn't have a lot of savvy. Part of his charm. But the real charm is letting go of however one defines *poetry,* as early readers of cummings had to do. Absorb the words (the stuff of poetry) in their idiosyncratic, often acolloquial, appearance: enter Hamilton's *Dreambox,* which comes directly from his poem, "Walkative, Talkative."

> Yet those are lines to another star
> That were to have been led by changelings
> Around a dark dreambox of another kind
> That houses our more talkative stars.

Hamilton was deep into metaphor, arguably living in metaphorland, often speaking in metaphor: "The mice have been nibbling my cheese" is how he explained why he had no milk, which had been pilfered from the group refrigerator that hummed from the first floor landing of his rooming house.

At first, Hamilton's publishing savvy was limited to stuffing three legal envelopes with fifteen one-page poems three times a week and mailing them to *Epoch,* Cornell University's national literary magazine, where they accumulated in shoeboxes, often unopened, three five-cent stamps the exact postage for each three-ounce envelope. No SASE. The poet David Ray, then on faculty and an *Epoch* editor, recognized Hamilton's genius and found a few poems to champion at editorial meetings. Some of them appear in *Epoch*s of the sixties and seventies.

David Ray brought a couple of Hamilton's fat legal envelopes to his Creative Writing 201 class, where I was among a dozen long-haired sophomores. He read a couple of the poems to the group and challenged us to explore new syntax, perhaps leading to fresh metaphor. Sitting next to David (we used his first name) at our big seminar table, I noticed the return address on those envelopes: Montclair, New Jersey. My hometown! During Christmas vacation, I stopped by unannounced at the return address and knocked on the big front door, which was answered by a man who pointed to Hamilton's room, right there on the left. "That's his room."

I knocked, and a moment later the door slid open, one of those doors on rollers that slides into the wall. Hamilton welcomed me with little apparent surprise, shook my hand, invited me in. The room smelled of pipe tobacco. He was then about fifty years old, but at least to this young man he appeared to be in his seventies. Balding, slight, stooped, gray. "Would you like some red daisies?" I was sitting on his cot. He was in the chair at the table that held his large manual typewriter and a ream of paper labeled *Sphinx.*

Sphinx

The sphinx said:
I wanted no hurt
I wanted no pain ever again
I wondered if that was all that was ever meant
And ever happened

"Red daisies"? Uh, yes. For sure! Back in David's class, we'd all marveled at one of the poems he had convinced his fellow editors to publish.

Liquid'll

For that's a pint of red daisies
That has been sent to your florist
That he has become your drunkard.

Yes, I'd love some red daisies. And out came a pint of Four Roses blended whiskey, a fingerful of which he poured into each of two milk glasses, handing one to me.

Wait 'til I got back to Cornell! I had the key to Hamilton's metaphor! At least to me this was a major breakthrough: you know, the kind that might inspire a PhD dissertation and later, a book! Likely to David Ray, and maybe most of my classmates, this was old news, but I felt I had the key to poetry. A breakthrough.

This sense of having discovered something special added fire to my reading of Alfred Starr Hamilton's poems. I absorbed the idiosyncratic syntax of the poems and experimented unsuccessfully in my own poems with Hamiltonian repetitions and incomplete phrases. Among my favorite Hamilton poems "April Lights," just seven lines, bursts into colloquial voice, jarring the reader from the dream state created by the first five lines:

April Lights

But nevertheless there are some other kinds of blue skies
Some other way of counting the summer clouds that stayed
There is the red moon, by October
Some other kind of February lights
Some other kind of January darkness that is deeper
A bronze rake –
A winding road to where we are this evening

Al seemed a humble and ultimately peaceful man, yet he was stubborn and held to unique principles. I was fascinated that he had been arrested in 1961 for refusing to seek shelter during an air raid drill, perhaps the town's first instance of civil disobedience. He notified the local police in advance with a letter, announcing in part: "Peaceably protesting the air raid siren on April 28, 4 P.M., I will be sitting in the park at Watchung Plaza by the flag pole, reasonably refusing shelter, that I will not resist being arrested impersonally, and may peaceably be taken to the station."

Hamilton held stubbornly to his own vision of poetry, writing "no collaboration" at the top of correspondence (intending to discourage editorial suggestions) and adding "D.D." to his typed signature. "Dishonorably Discharged," he explained, during one of the dozen or so times I dropped by when I was back in town. As a pacifist, he took pride in the "dishonorably," and in his letters, he frequently addressed the "honorable" with disapproval— "Doesn't make such a great deal of difference, but I fear honorable deliberations. I don't accept literary honors."

My visits were few and scattered over the years, the last probably in 2000. There was a sameness to these visits, though I don't recall any red daisies after the first; perhaps he reserved them for introductions only. It was mice in the cheese on our third or fourth meeting, and other metaphorical statements that I wish I'd jotted down. I'm sure he liked having company; we almost always talked about his daily routine and the fruits of his growing notoriety. By the 1980s poets were corresponding with him, editors were requesting new poems, a couple of colleges had invited him to give readings: his work and his legend were spreading!

When I last stopped by, Al had moved, and the man who answered the door did not know where. Months later I discovered that he was in a nursing home; I telephoned and learned that he had died.

In an article I wrote in 1965 for Cornell's undergraduate literary magazine, *The Trojan Horse,* I likened reading Hamilton's poems to visiting an art museum. One pauses to study a few of the works in a museum, and breezes past others. Entering Hamilton's dreambox is easiest when one feels no obligation to dwell on each "work of art," but seeks the one in ten or twenty that imparts a smile of recognition or chills with stark surprise. As with my discovery of The Key to Metaphor, this smile or chill can open the way to greater appreciation of some of the skimmed poems, eventually spreading like red daisies on a white carpet until the whole thing's been soaked.

Slow Parlor

Are you afraid of time?
Are you afraid of the clock
That unwinds itself in the slow parlor?
Do you know of a drop of rain
That falls on the spindle?
Are you a friend of a box of dark June roses?
Do you know of the pendulum
That swings to the June chimes?

With gratitude to Ben Estes and Alan Felsenthal for bringing us this vibrant collection!

GEOF HEWITT
CALAIS, VT

A Dark Dreambox of Another Kind

SWAN IN JUNE

The moon is a swan in June
The moon can paddle and paddle
And be the moon all night long

LITTLE

aren't we all lifelike?
Those are the thuds of thunder
at the back of our bones
aren't we all moonlike?
Those are the buds of thunder
by our glassified gravestones
aren't we all ready
for those last moonlike promises?
aren't we all being a little talkative as yet?
for those buds of thunder
at the back of our moonlike bones

LITTLE NEWS

and strings of fire are welcome,
but I burned to hear the news,
in a minute, that's a golden linnet,
that's a snug little faery canary
that'll whistle the song of David
that sped to your silvery hearts,
little news

SNOWFLAKE

Wait till I see myself
At the October Looking Glass

That is a spool of silver
That winds itself through
The autumnal Looking Glass

That winds itself through
And during more of November
And through and throughout
The first November snowflake

GUEST OF THE MONTH OF MAINE

Maybe we found another word in the mist
Maybe we found another cucumber during our garden travels
Maybe we found another word for bluebird
That flew higher and higher up in the blue sky
Maybe we found another gray cloud somewhere
Where sheep gathered in the prolonged mist
Maybe we were all poets today and tomorrow
Maybe we found another word for a bluebird
That flew over a gray cloud in the distance

SPHINX

The sphinx said:
I wanted no hurt
I wanted no pain ever again
I wondered if that was all that was ever meant
And ever happened

KATYDIDS

I wondered if I were restless
and katy did it
and katy did it some moreso
and all the while I did what katy did
and katy dotted my drifting i's
and crossed my bewildered t's
and katy answered all my revolutionary questions
and katy told me no lies the world over
and katy wondered for me
and katy wondered if I were restless
and katy lived in a village
and katy and you and I tilled the soil
and katy and you and I wandered
no further than the village door

CINDERELLA

were you ever a little reindeer
out in the clear
not too tiny a reindeer
but a little reindeer
and the way was clear

were you ever a little reindeer
out in the rain
not a big rain
but a little rain
and the way was clear

and you had your umbrella with you
not too big an umbrella
but a little umbrella
and your name was Cinderella

wonderfully you were invited
to a ceremony
not too big a ball
but a little ball
and you had your umbrella with you

RHYME SHOT

Oh, that's an old French horsefly
That rode around an elastic
And still is going to bite
Everyone over the Xmas holidays

I could have done either, –
Finally I wrote to the governor of poetry
And simply signed my own name

THAT FIXED YOUR WINDPIPE

A blubbery way of talking
But what is needed mostly
Is a blubbery handkerchief
For blowing your blubbery nose
If you were a balloon tire of a fellow
For a cold January rose

BLACK AND GOLD

Are words formed out of a Hades kind of delight?
Some are softer, Some are fonder, some are horrid;
In black dreamland I know of others' stars,
An angel hammers, another bids him horrid harder,
And raw stars, and raw words, some are sorcerous fonder
Of raw ends of Black's pounding golden laughter;
Stars fly, an angel bids harder and founder
Of Smith's dreamland; I know of others' stars,
Words are formed out of torrid Times of golden nights

SLOW PARLOR

Are you afraid of time?
Are you afraid of the clock
That unwinds itself in the slow parlor?
Do you know of a drop of rain
That falls on the spindle?
Are you a friend of a box of dark June roses?
Do you know of the pendulum
That swings to the June chimes?

APRIL LIGHTS

But nevertheless there are some other kinds of blue skies
Some other way of counting the summer clouds that stayed

There is the red moon, by October

Some other kind of February lights
Some other kind of January darkness that is deeper

A bronze rake –
A winding road to where we are this evening

NEIGHBORS

Why didn't you say a pumpkin on top of the wall?
Over election day, afterwards,
And hand your neighbor another pumpkin
Why didn't you mean pumpkin pie?
To have been with the crust of what is the matter
How could you have been the slough of despond
That skulked in the pasture?

YES

I know of drawing the line
I know of a bar of Iron at the looking glass
I know of a boy who is bowing his head
I know of a boy who is learning how to say yes
I know of a boy who is learning how
to ty his own bowty

POOR

being poor
over the bare pavements

being poor
over a bare floor

until as ever there is something
left there to be had

APPLE

To have caught the ripe thread
To an apple is your wishing well
Why, the water is like silver wine, to one,
For silver lakes are full of silver wells
To a lonely lake dining over October

BRONZE CHIMES

I wanted the bronze chimes
    in the sunset
I wanted the last autumn leaves
    that clung to the trees
To have gathered what little there is left
    of the midday sunshine
But I wanted the wishing well
During the last of our autumn travels
I wanted to have run to the corduroy sunset
    in the gloaming
I wanted to have climbed the enchanted forest stairway
But I wanted to have tossed a penny's worth
Back into the Indian wishing well
That held our wonderful hopes

SUNSETS

Are you a golden blonde?,
Are you a silver blonde?
Who believes in the man who tends to the sunsets

Do you believe in a train of daily thunder,
Do you believe in a stoker
That stokes the daily fires
That is diving downwards!

Are you a golden blonde?
Are you a silver blonde?
Do you believe in the man who built the moon?,
Who constructed thunder out of a blade of grass

GOLD STANDARD

Gold is your friend
But gold starves you
And I and others
For lack of gold

Why didn't we take our golden chances?
Why didn't we liken ourselves for gold?
And stay at the Indian sundial
And count the wonderful chimes

SUMMER

even time slept on
a leaf for how long
and stole away time

even time came to be
a bud for how long
and asked for time

even a bud came to be
a leaf for how long
and asked for more time

even time stayed at a sundial for how long
and counted its evening feathers then left

SEDGE

A little sedge twilight is important
in the life of an artist

on the other hand
a sedge worm
is a cruel crocodile tear
that should never have been
for your diamond ring

GOOD BOOK

If their path was one of desire
Where is their desire in this land of miles upon miles
Of waste? – of bitter black cold loneliness
Gray packs of them streak through the silent night
One can hear them, one cannot spot one of them,
Day and night, night and day, leaps and bounds on
Endlessly towards where is one's desire, why is one's desire?
Where there is no desire or end to desire or lure
Of dread, depth, or breadth of miles, Of one lone wolf howl
In this land of black cold on white loneliness
And days one builds one's fire in that wonderful loneliness
Days of waiting, watching, of glued glassified city wondering
Of wandering by one's thoughts, how I loved loneliness, or moreover

DARK ANGEL

Tomorrow night I walked to a dark black star
That I can have uncovered the face of the moon

Today and tonight I walked to a seventh noon star in heaven
That I opened the face of heaven, that I counted the dark chimes

I walked along the pathway of a black butterfly
I entered the forest of dark bewilderment

Either the other half of the black star that blinds the moon
Was lifted to the moon on either wing of the noon butterfly

That is a dark angel during the spool of black thread
That unwinds the moon that pulls the wheels of time

TOMORROW

Those are the blossoms under the branches
That have been picked, but would have been left there
Those are the broken stars at the back of the wonderbrush
Those are the stars that were kept to put on top of the daisy tops
Tomorrow and next day, and all summer long
Those are the hushabye places as long as ever remembered
Still those are the timelier visions remembered
I never said goodbye to the broken places under the branches
That was all we were ever meant to be to ourselves, Tomorrow

A CRUST OF BREAD

why, I often wondered
why I was a poet,
first of all

most of all, I wanted
to have been a bird
if I could have been a bird

but I wanted the starlings
to have been fed,
first of all

THE POOL

I never played pool with all the rest
I was so oftentimes off by myself
I didn't know what it was
I didn't know where it was
It never left me alone
It spoke to me time and again
I stared at the pool
I stared at the beautiful face of mankind
And there it was at the bottom of the pool,
One of the clearest dreams I've ever witnessed
A little crawfish at the bottom of the pool,
A little crawfish on top of a sandy beach,
I could have that little thingamajig
I could hug that little thingamajig to myself all of the rest of my
    life long

PINK BIRDS

Somehow, these were the pink stonewalls
That were never to have been climbed
More than ever more pink birds
Flew over into one anothers' pastures
But they all wore mourning stonewall faces
They tried to talk to one another
But it never rained on their parched tongues, they were tongue tied,
They built one parched stonewall on top of another
To have prevented the blink birds from falling on the crops
Speechlessly, they faced their own deaf stonewalls
To have put one toadstool on top of another
To have built the pink tower of Babel

SHOTGUN

During Chicago
I shot a shotgun
That outlasted a pistol
That should have been
A spade and a shovel
For shoveling Chicago

CROSSROADS

yet I walked through the gay city of November
in search of the word for a snowflake
that stayed on a man's overcoat
for I searched the gray winds for none other answer
than I'll never know whyever
I lived at a crossroads of conclusions
for I concluded
that I lit an amber lamp alone in the parlorways

OH GIVE US THE STORM!

Oh, give us back our thunder
Oh, give us a beach that has been lashed
By rain and quick gusts of salt winds
Oh, give us the storm!
But, Oh give us again the sailor
Who'll wait for the turn of the ocean tides
Oh, give us an ocean that is full of stars
Oh, give us time, nor change of winds,
And save us the sailor past Little Rock
Who'll sail homeward with the change of one tide
Oh, give us ever again
A sedge hammer that has been thrown to the moon

PSYCHE

but I don't know
however it felt more like
scraping one's spareribs
for whatever is left of
the moon at the bottom of the pan

MOON AND STARS

I thought of its hindsight
I thought of its foresight
I thought it was wearing its eyes on the back of its head
I thought its eyes were everywhere
I thought it was star gazing
I thought it was staring upwards
I thought of such dizzying heights
I thought this was upside down
I thought it was observing the underworld
I thought it was observing the wilderness
I thought the stars were on fire
I thought it was observing the moon
I thought it was funny
I thought the moon was for some pumpkin

FOR A FIREFLY

if ever
an evening star

JANUARY PARLOR

But a snowflake stayed on one's lips
I talked to a golden jar of white roses
That stayed in the January parlor

TOWN RACE

Magnetically to have cornered a star
That stuck in a town's dark throat
That thundered, that it talked to fast time

even magic steel that pushed the pushbutton
that kept the town ecstatically bound together

Fast as it fled to a stealthier angel
To have entered the bulb in the parlor

SCHOOLHOUSE

I would
If I could
I would like
To do anything for you
As light as the moon
I would like
To go over the green pastures
From then on to follow
This is for the green leaves
This is for the yellow leaves
This is for a little green and yellow schoolhouse
By the forsythia hillside
To tell you the truth
If I only could

I would like to write the history of our lives over again
I would like to build you a little Indian schoolhouse
I would like to send you a box of daffodils too
Considering the lilies of the valley
And neither do they spin nor do they toil
And send them back to school

RECLUSE

Oh, tho, I know now whyever the moon is a recluse
Oh, tho, I know now the best things there are to be had are secluded
Oh, tho, I know now of the nymphs there are
Oh, tho, I know now of the angels there are
And tonight the nymphs are dreaming of the angels
And tonight the angels are dreaming of the nymphs

DUSTY ANYTHING

Even I wanted to be a speck of dusty anything
That wore spectacles over a clover blossom

Even I wanted to have hummed less handsomely
Than a sword that has been thrown at a cloudlike being

But I wanted to be a summer angel
That worked with the plow over the blossom
That hummed with the faery summer winds

PURSUIT UPON HAPPINESS

Oh mad pursuit upon happiness
And when the day is ended – and there is none
Thy dreams are on fire in the searching sunsets
That have burned upon the sands of thine own kinds of times
Thy youth was full of glass charms, of daydreams
Upon cases, One's heart is overflowing of fair faith
One's midday cactus bloom in under the scorching sun
One's midday pursuit after happiness, and what elderly years
Are last few leaves are on fire in the scorching sunsets
Although unhappily before thy trek is done

DARK CONTINENT

What do you know of its players
What do you know of its populations
What do you know of this amber theatre
What do you know of this dark continent
What do you know of its wintry cities
What do you know of St. Johns
What do you know of New York
What do you know of its glamour
What do you know of its short aptitudes
What do you know of city lights
What do you know of its urge
What do you know of its fast bubbles on the surface
What do you know of its orange contempt

DARK CORNER

I wonder if I lived
in a dark corner
all by myself
until the only sun I ever saw
came around in the morning
I wonder if the sunlight
worked its way
through a keyhole
and little by little I was taught
never to tell a lie
I wonder of how the light of day
exerted itself
in my presence

TAMPA, FLORIDA

To sting a centipede around
A pineapple bend, on a peach – truth is
Studied on the breast – abysmally

A picture of a tramp is being excruciated
Betwixt a splintered parked bent bench

And truthfully
And in Africa
A pink pygmy
Sits stupidly on a bamboo spear
In the hark wide open jungle

THURSDAY

Couldn't you have waited for the gold there was on Thursday
Couldn't you have waited for how little gold there was to be had
It rained on Tuesday
It rained again on Wednesday
The sun came behind the clouds that little on Thursday
The sky was blustery and overcast
There was a halo and the purple and the gold

A CARROT

I wanted to find a little yellow candlelight in the garden

DIDN'T YOU EVER SEARCH FOR ANOTHER STAR?

I.

did you say
August ponds
ought to have
been surrounded
by September fences?

but did you say
September fences
ought to have
been climbed over
by October peoples?

what did you say
for October padlocks
that ought never to have
been attached moreover
to November handcuffs?

II.

You'll remember us for our dark Hungarian laughter
That tickled when it laughed, that dug at the limelight

Why, I'll send you a dark silver Hungarian coin
From the mines that never saw the light of day yet

Why, I'll send you a dime's worth of Hungarian damage
That has been done to a cave that is full of Rhapsody

Why, I'll send you a silver key to the cave of despair
I'll send you a violet tonight, I'll send you a silver sword

I'll send you a silver hammer that'll hammer night and day
I'll send you a pail-ful of our kinds of blue revolutionary stars

III.
Who are you? Weren't you their prisoner in the sedge dark?
Where has been your search for freedom?
Will you count the trees again in these dense woods
Wherever you have been tonight?
Will you look backwards where you have been?
And tell me whoever you are.
What have been your escapes?
Nevertheless freedom is as ever an intense girl angel
That speaks to one in the inane wilderness
Where has been your phantasmagoria?
Are the dark trees at war with the darklike trees?
Where has been your light
Where has been your swordy well,
Where has been your darklike table?
Didn't you ever search for another star?

SCOTCH

Scotch is reasonable
That lifted some fog
Over a bar of ice

DAFFODILS

I wanted the golden birds of paradise
To have flown to the race of mankind

I wanted the golden boat of friendship
To have been for the four golden masts to the sun

Sailing this side of laughter to a cloud
Living under the seventh star of heaven for freedom

I wanted you and I to have been pervaded
By the sun for the winged notes of peace

But I wanted the laughter of the men on board
To have been with the four daffodils of the seas

I wanted all else safe and sound on board,
That is said by an architect, I wanted no lies ever again

SNOW FLOWERS

When those are the daffodils at the window sill
Those are the snowflakes that flew with the sun's new drifts
Afterwards those are the daffodil drawers
Until the time came to be gruff winter
Wherever they'd kept their winter clothing
Neatly tucked away in the bureau drawers
But those are the ice cold wintry snow flowers
That drifted over the daffodil hours that pushed the snow plow
That visited the snowman through the white and drifting snow

DIME

The hardest travels I ever had were on the king's highway
The hardest travels I ever had were over the dusty roads
The hardest script I ever wrote of was over a diamond
I pushed a plow over thine kingdom come of events
I pushed a plow over the face of a dime

WHEAT METROPOLIS

Isn't this grinding the valves a little closer to your ears
Isn't this grinding the wheat that was noticed against the running board
Isn't this living a little nearer to the center of activity
Isn't this wonderful taking a car out west
Or taking a bus and all your elephantine belongings
And running as fast as your legs can carry you
Isn't this wonderful noticing the wheat against your windshield
Isn't this a yearling
Isn't this a slender reed
Isn't the corn a little green behind the ears
Isn't this a little affrighted
Isn't this daredeviltry of another kind
On a nickel or a dime
Or hitchhiking or nonetheless

VINELIKE

even a green leaf
turned and toiled

and said to the twig
that turned to the trunk

at length that pulled at the living roots of the matter
that pulled and toiled to the end of its vinelike travels

THE PAPERMILL PLAYHOUSE

nevertheless I've got a little stereo pencil
that goes, and it goes, and it goes like a little
car around town, and it stops, and it starts, and
it sputters, and it goes again, and it goes, and
it goes, and it goes, and it goes uphill, and it
goes downhill, and it goes around and around, and
it stops at all the stop signs where there are
policemen, and it goes to the opera, and it goes
to the papermill playhouse, where there are players,
where there are heroes and heroines, where there are
flags and flagellations, where there are servants
of old, where there are lessons, where there is old
king Wenceslas, where there are foresters of yore
gathering winter fuel, and it goes to entertainments
and holiday festivals, and so it goes, and it goes
over the hill, and it goes uptown, and it goes down-
town, and around town, and it goes to the schoolhouse.
and it goes to the grocery store, and it marks down
groceries, and it goes to the station where there are
train whistles, and it goes, and it starts, and it
sputters, and it goes again, and it goes, and it goes,
and it goes.

XERXES

it was all so Xerxes the other night
the path they travelled was so slender
the bridge they were crossing was being
torn asunder by the storm, and I in my
bonnet was sound asleep, and
the bullywhip of the winds and the storm
lashed the troops of Xerxes, and
Xerxes in his rage ordered the river
itself to be lashed back, and the river
responded, and the storm abated, and all
was as calm as ever, and the engineers
returned to their work

WALDEN HOUSE

Are you a fierce nomad?
Are you a friend of sword and disaster?
Do you know of the only star in heaven?
Do you know of only the sun's daily sword
That pushed the scorched wagon wheels forward?
Are you a goldhunter?
Are you a Scythian mountebank?
Are you a plainsman who fled the plains?
Will you recross the deserted desert airways?
Or are you a Walden traveler?
Do you have your meals at the Walden House?
Do you read your wanton heels to your shoemaker?
Are you a city traveler?

WALDEN HOUSE

during my Walden pencil
tall buildings followed me downstairs
upstairs the truth blossomed
the wind caught in its city branches
the blue cold glistened
on top of one cloud,
windwards, and ever withinwards,
for I pulled my blue coat over my Subway sleeve

TOWN

Give us time
Give us crickets
Give us a clock
could you build this wonderful town house in the grass
and put a cricket in it by this evening?

DAFFODILS

Those are waterfalls to be forgiven
But those are mountains of laughter
Those are plain tales of the mountainous moon
I wanted daffodils to have been picked off of the moon
But I wanted the laughter of the girls
Who gathered the daffodils in the starlight
For those are the silhouettes in the lingering darkness
That lifted our yellow pencils to have told the tale tonight
Of the man who laughed on top of the moon

JANUARY GALLERY

Did you say today?
Did you say tomorrow,
Or the next day, or the day afterwards?
Did you say a picture at a January gallery?
Did you say a glass eye for your mirror
For a club foot for a clump of wintery woods?,
For a little of lavender that stares back at you
Today and tomorrow, and days afterwards

WHITE CHIMES

Gin is white, for a white while,
And of its soft white dreams
One pillows oneself;
One softens of oneself,
Comfortably one mirrors oneself;
More comfortably one's soft white dreams
Are more to do with Time, softspoken,
One loves wafting oneself away of soft chimes

HOME OR ABROAD

Why didn't you say the stars were in her eyes
Why didn't you say the cloud was over a sun
Why didn't you say every cloud has a silver lining
Why didn't you say the sun comes shining through
Why didn't you say you were for peace

Why didn't you stay home
Why didn't you say there was thunder over the grass
Why didn't you count the stumbling blocks over again
Why didn't you say your elbow was on fire
Why didn't you say you were for freedom

Why didn't you say you were stupefied
Why didn't you say you were dumbfounded
Why weren't you confounded
Why didn't you say the sun was for the looking glass
Why didn't you say a cloud just now has passed over the looking glass

MARY O'ROONEY

Are you swept daily at a Looking Glass?
Have you your books at a bookshelf
That stared back at you?, That you came upon
A stairway that led three flights upstairs
Are you contented if you ever could be?
Are you a member of a dark room?, swept daily

CHRISTMAS EVE

I wondered once if they were going
To put a very skimpy tree in the parlor
I wondered of the floor wax over the bare floor
I knew this was going to be a very slim Christmas
But I knew they were very poor people
I wondered if I put a diamond on top of a paper dollie
I wondered if that's all I could do too

THAT STAYS WITH US ABROAD

Oh, give us a star
    That is to be found in the wanton wheat fields
        That have roamed with the summer winds

Oh, give us that light
    That lifted the golden moon
        On top of the haystack stairway

Oh, give us the word
    For our flag that is the golden corn
        That waves wonderfully in the summer breezes abroad

But, give us the sun
    That stays with us abroad on our broad backs
        During our overland daily travels

FRAMEWORK

Of the November Framework
Squirrels ran along the bare November branches
But a tree is an amber stairway
That is being hammered during November
for the reminder of a daily architectural hammer
That stays with the autumn framework

OF SUCH SUN STUFF

of such sun stuff
that sang the merrier tunes
for the golden canary bird
that traversed the sunlight
throughout the morning parlor

nevertheless one's fears
are made of such sun stuff
that are a tiger's burning brands in the darkening jungle
that discovered the golden beetle
that flew to the voice of gunpowder
that destroyed the summer harvests
that flew to tyrannical commands in the boom distance
that wanted only the roar of the light of day

INDIAN, AND HARVARD

Even September screens
    That kept the last August flies out of the parlor
        That kept their August greens on top of the bookshelves

though, Good News for the Indian Harvard bugs
That kept their September fingers onto the pages of cotton –

tails, But you'll remember us most of all
    To the first Indian August cottonpicker that lifted
        The avalanche of cotton for the Indian summer holidays

.SING .SING

was it a bud at the back of the bosom
that bled and bled all summer long?

was it still a bud at the back of the vine
that came to bloom in June?, but bled

was it a white carnation flower
in July that held itself closer to the vine?

was it a button on a man's shirt
that shall have been sewed and seared nearer to the vine?

was it your love?
was it my love?
was it your love fled?
was it a cloud in the summer sky?

was it you and I and everyone, and Tonio
who knew of a deeper lexicon wound
during August, and onto July?

was it a voice in August?
was it a summer voice?
and do you remember?

yet and all was it an arrested rose in September?, to bloom,
that stayed at its rocking chair, persisted of itself closer to the vine

OCTOBER ALE

October wine is for an October ale
That is being served over the frost
That has been left with an apple

BOOKS

lend us a scholarly hand
    over the oil for the lamps of China

lend us time
    lend us rags for wonderful pleasures
lend us a bookshelf

lend us a little care
    with the scholarly Aladdin

who wished for fewer leaves for earnings
who wished for more books for buttonhooks
on the reasonable bookshelf

over the burning autumnal dusks

JUDITH AND HER MAIDSERVANT

For they walked for miles
For they walked for days
For they walked for months
For they walked for bloody ages in the wilderness
For they stumbled upon castles
For they stumbled upon larger jewelry
For they stumbled upon rubies
For they stumbled upon the largest rube of all
For they stumbled upon the excruciating rube of time
This was theirs for the asking tho they refused
For they stumbled upon folds of rhinoceri who knew no better
    than ants
For they stumbled upon bearded giants
For they stumbled upon bloodshot eyes
For they stumbled upon peoples who had lost their countenance
For they stumbled upon peoples who had lost their taste and savor
For they stumbled upon family aptitude for spiders an inch longer
For they stumbled upon children who were boys or girls or either
For they carried the gore's head a step farther at a time
For they were on their way past these heaps of humid affluence
Still they followed the thin trickle of a stream for some or a few violets
For they were on their way toward the civilized forests

FOR ALL I KNOW

for all I know
    someone else said that

"A black cricket
That stays at a black thicket
Is for later August"

for all I know
    someone else said that
lake waters are thirstier
    for some other kinds of August stars

WALKATIVE, TALKATIVE

When those are the walkative stars
That talked to the immediate prisoners themselves
When those are the talkative stars
That walked along the narrow sedge pathways
Yet those are lines to another star
That were to have been led for changelings
Around a dark dreambox of another kind
That houses our more talkative stars

GOLD ON THE MOON

I'll mourn the gold on the moon a day longer
I'll mourn the gold on my sleeve a day further
I'll delay the passing away of time
I'll live to sing a lullaby of the moon
I'll mourn all of my wonderful belongings
That have withered since yesterday and today

OLD SONGS

Take me back to the days
of why I talked to the moon
Of the immoveable church
When we moved
But the church was immoveable
But the church was your neighbor

Take me back to the days
Of an old walnetto song
To a walnetto blonde
That pinned the white blossoms over the blossom,
and pulled at the heart's strings of the world

That said your best heart
Is your neighbor of old

SILVER POET

everlastingly stronger
on top of the moon
I wanted no stranger being
to have been tied
to a silver string
that is said of the voice of an angel
and in the moonlight
I wanted a man
to have been a silver poet

FAT CINCH

On a cinch
On a dime
When you're twenty

On a pinch
On a dime
When you're forty

On a moon ride
On a Hay ride

It isn't a cinch
On a dime
When you're flat fifty

BUBBLE GUM

More like a rubber check
More like a rubber ball
More like a rubbery war salad
More like having the same salad over again

LITTLE SWORD

put the moon for the sphere
back in the tobacco jar

but some of these swollen spheres
were to have been worded by swollen angels,
yet to have been pierced by the little sword!

THE BOOK OF NUMBERS

I wonder if you knew more of soft lights in the garden
I wonder if you knew more of amber lights in the parlors
I wonder if you knew more of the Jack-O-Lanterns
I wonder if you knew more of the umbrellas
That are hung on the racks every time it rained
I wonder if you knew more of straw hats
That are hung by the chimney with care
I wonder if you knew more of a soft summer's night
I wonder if you knew more of the book of numbers
I wonder if you knew more of facts and figures
I wonder if you knew more of affording a ford
I wonder if you knew more of the diamond in the wheat
I wonder if you knew more of the University of Camden
I wonder if you knew more of excommunications
I wonder if you knew more of tour-a-lie
I wonder if you knew more of Point Lookout
Of a race of bishops and savages many moon miles away

DOMINOES

A poet is a ranger
A poet is a ranger who found a star
A poet is far reaching
A poet is an explorer
Who discovered the house on top of the moon
To have built the topsy turvy house
A poet is a parlor ranger
Who wanted to put more stars before other stars
And called that a game of dominoes

NIGHT

I kept a typewriter
I carried a little dark suitcase around
I asked the proprietor for some or a little space
I was a stranger
I was always moving about
I knew there was lightning on the moon
I hammered golden letters against the wilderness
I hammered golden letters against the night
I held this light to myself
I had so little to say to all the rest

DIM GOLD

Dark violin music plays over
Some dim gold letters tonight
That are kept in your hat

PEACE BEING

Morning's dishwashing isn't as golden to some,
If others have their afternoon's golden noonish
And golden sun's in the east side's kitchen windows,
And golden suds, and golden sun's suds are rarer
If the morning's fresh and full of Saturday's dishpans,
Peace being, frying pans, that do belong, to be scraped,—
Truth is there are afternoon's Saturday children to be scraped;
Knees that are scraped, those that shine, those that are dirtier,
And heroes that hid behind fire escapes, those are dirtier than
    others,—
And sunshine in suds does live in the minds of golden mothers
Out of afternoonish golden west side kitchen windows,
Outlandishly, they couldn't be scraped, they can't be scraped,
They will never be scraped or cleaned or gilded forever

SUMMER

Why didn't you say an inkstand
Why didn't you say all of this was for the blue sky
Why didn't you say a sheet of writing paper was for a cloud

IRK

ink came to you and I
in the middle of the night
over the sheets
if you meant ink
if you meant an inkling
if you meant a crayon
if you meant a cave
if you meant a cave man
if you needed ink
if you needed coal,
upon my soul

SKY AND PURPOSES

I know this is colossal
I know this is possible
I know I can do it
I know I can do it again
I know I can do it again and again
I know of a big cloud that is shaped for an elephant
I know of a little cloud that is shaped for a peanut
I know of pushing the little cloud over to the big cloud
I know of putting the peanut onto the elephant's trunk

AN APPLE, ORGANIZATIONALLY

An ache in the back of the eyeballs some,
    and how that was never to have befriended an object

And objects came to be justified
    that they had no life or meaning

Except to be judged daynight and tomorrow

And little by little these came to be objects everywhere,
    and counted clouds, and objects came to be clouds

THE CARDINAL IN THE BUSH

I wanted to know more about the cardinal
I wanted to know more about what the cardinal did
I wanted to know more about the cardinal in the bush

I wanted to know more about what the cardinal said to the cricket
I wanted to know more about what the cricket said to the cardinal
I wanted to know more about the cardinal in the bush

I wanted to know more about what Frere Jacques said
I wanted to know more about what Frere Jacques said to the cardinal
I wanted to know more about the cricket in the bush

I wanted to know more about what the cricket said
I wanted to know more about the light of the silvery moon
I wanted to know more about those little white lies

I wanted to know more about a fair day
I wanted to know more about a fair night
I wanted to know more about tickets to the fair

FOR MOUNT MONADNOCK

(mountain in N.H. that is made of solid rock)

well, I wondered over
the isinglass over rocks
and counted the rocks that wound the watchword
over the isinglass that leapt over your locks and keys
that I came to the pith of the New Hampshire matter, finally,
for your rocks on top of your elbow beams
stitch the golden music

RIDE

for this has been our last bequest
how little do you know of our old fashioned silver spoons
how little do you know of the snowflake in the jar
how little do you know of the ride in the valley
how little do you know of the thread that rides
through and through our old fashioned silver spoons
how little do you know of our painstaking over the years
how little do you know of the donkey on the end of a spoon
happily, how little do you know of preserving our sedge
we are only bled and gone

BREAD AND BUTTER

for I always preferred the kinds of claws
that found nothing in the Wilderness
that crawled further over the pavements
that were less fearsome of the light of day
they thought less of bread and butter over their paws
they wandered further from the hovels of all the rest

TENNESSEE

Those are our white fables
Those are our black fables
Those are some of our earliest American fables
Those are the northernmost fables of Lief Ericksen
But those are the southernmost fables of some of our greatest ancestors
They proceed from the tip of South America
They knew less of heed and encounter
They proceeded further northward
They proceeded over the General American plains
Those are some of our earliest American travelers
Those are some of our earliest American settlers
Those are some of our earliest American explorers

EVEN THE DEEP SEA

Even the deep sea
Laughs at a day of despair

ANYTHING REMEMBERED

One cloud, one day
Came as a shadow in my life
And then left, and came back again; and stayed

BLIZZARD

moreover
creeps over
the barren astonished earth
moreover that is a cat's white velvet claw
that can have been named after the white and drifting snow

CRABAPPLES

Why didn't you know of a hurt?
Words
hurt
If
I
never spoke
to you

about a hard apple
that can have been gobbled
and gobbled some more and

about a rooster

that clutched at the truth's breast
that can have clawed and clawed
at the good earth
that can never have been yourself

who never hurt
who never knew

of an idiot poet of your own hard kind and breeding
who ate dyspepsia for bread

SHEETS

How wonderfully the moon was to have been ironed last night
And carefully kept the moon in its place
And last night I ironed the moon
And lifted the daffodil back on top of the daisy
And folded the daffodil back on top of the moon
And carefully carried the moon upstairs
And kept the moon in the daffodil closet
Last time I ironed the moon

IRONING BOARD

Ironically, an iron bud
    blooms in the summer heat

Ironically, an iron bunny
    speaks to one at a summer sunset window

They never read of the bitter toilsome roots
    of the summer daisies that swayed in the sunset winds

They never knew of the daisies at the table
    but an iron bud smoothes them over carefully

        "puts one daisy for one wise guy
            after another into a basket, and keeps one
            daisy ironed for oneself Tonight
            that roams crazily at the dumb doorway"

Yet as ever a daylong roaming bunny
    speaks wisely of Today's travels, at sunset range

BON VIVRE

Vivre, Vivre,
Don't live forever, Vivre,
Good livers don't live forever, Vivre,

Stars don't,
We don't,

Live forever, sharpen ourselves,
For a magnificent eternal occasion

And of an occasion
I saw one star fading

It bid itself, Vivre,
Candled itself, Handled itself,
For must it stay lit forever
On the eternally magnificent bitter black nights?

LIQUID'LL

That's a pint of red daisies
That has been sent to your florist
That he has become your drunkard

GO AHEAD

Go ahead, if it's raining on a January morning
Go ahead, and put the daffodils on the pavements
Go ahead, and sing us a song
Go ahead, and ring us on the phone
Live this rainstorm down, if you only could
Live this down to the shining pavements
Go ahead, and gather the daffodils off of the night

PETER PILTDOWN

"I was poor
I was this simple person
I revered
I was reverent
I revered postage stamps
I revered my poverty
I revered my miseries
I ventured beautific dreams
I ventured enchantments
I ventured further than I could
I ventured delusions
I revered Peter Piltdown
Peter Piltdown was a fairy priest
I revered these poorer districts
I revered tall tenement houses
I revered steeples
I revered the places Peter Piltdown had ever been
I revered Peter Piltdown
I revered his celestial garments
Peter Piltdown came to visit me that once
And left these flowers in a vase
I revered these flowers
I remember my poverty"

VINEGAR BEND

Why didn't you say Vinegar
If they wanted Vinegar
For the flag that waved slovenly at Vinegar Bend

and lifted the tilted flagpole
and scoured the pastor's gospel of rage
and scrubbed the flagstone good and properly
and worked their hands in the grime and oil

And sent the flag to the cleaners,
And anything of the nature of Vinegar
For the flag that fluttered at Vinegar Bend

NEGRO SERGEANT

That is all that is to be said of a blacksnake
That shone and shone like black shoeleather
That scoured a gun under a sour blue sky

THE FLAG

What bright crops!
What bright harvests!
What bright jewels!
What bright acres!
What bright plains!
What a bright continent!
What bright Wisconsin trails!
What bright trails through the forests!
What bright sunshiny lakes!
What bright mountains ahead of ourselves!
What bright destinations!
What bright shining seas!
What bright waves that have been pounding our coasts!
What a bright clear day!
What do you know of the glow of the scorpion fly?
What do you know of the trail across the sky?
What do you know of the spidrex throwing the anchor?
What do you know of the spidrex throwing the light?
What do you know of the spidrex sewing the stars across the blue
    azure?
What do you know of the wonderful stripes?
What do you know of the beautiful ribbons of light?
What do you know of what beautiful red and white stripes?
What do you know of the thread of the scorpion?
What do you know of the scorpion that rests in our flag?

LITTLE IS TO BE SAID

little is to be said
Over tomorrow

little is to be said
Over today

little is to be said
Over a raindrop

little is to be said
Over a parade bearing a casket

little is to be said
    Over yesterday's particle of a parade

I AKEWELL

I once had a mind
Like a little butterfly
That floated away in the silvery distance

Once upon a time
I wandered over to a nymph
During the stiff autumn sunshine

Still I wanted a mind
Wrapped up in a soft cocoon of hope
And never to despair

Yet and all over time
What the nymph said to me
That wove the vine of time and hush and sunshine

Yet once upon a time
I wanted to have been a butterfly
That floated away in the lake distance

AT THE ZOO

On the back of an invoice
I wrote my name in large Capitalist June Blue Letters

And because money was involved
And so was my name ever in jeopardy

On the back of the same invoice
I rewrote my name in large Capitalist June Blue Letters

And in Leopardy and in Jeopardy
I resolved, dissolved upon a radical eradicator

Inking in, dissolving upon
Jeopardizing my own name in large Capitalist June Blue Letters

FOR YOUR PINK CHIPS

That's a rose colored cloud
That hovers over a war bank
That is high backed up against a blue sky
That is stacked higher
And is being covered

OCEAN

Gloom green spreads her white cloak
Along the shorelines – Picks up her laughter,
Fraught of lambs and starts of laughter,
Spreads her glee along the coastal lines

Gloom green spreads her white cloak
Along the shorelines – Flips her skirts that little
Folds it carefully, Tides it for awhile, Though
Recovers it gently, Riffles and Rumples itself
And back against the oncoming green gloom beautiful

THOU HAST COMMANDED THEM IN THEIR SLEEP

Deep in their sleep
Soldiers in their sleep
And Bo Peep and I
Can count of the number of sheep

On the number of sheep
And Bo Peep keeps an eye
Of the discipline of kinds of sheep

Some baa back sheep
And I closed an eye
On the number of kinds of sheep

At the number of sheep
And I opened an eye
Beating of the counting of sheep

Baa beating sheep
And Bo keeps an eye
Of the discipline of kinds of sheep

Sheep bumble backwards softly
Others baa forwards loudly
Humbly, softly, baa noisily

Some baa forwards
Others bleat backwards
I can count forwards
Eye can count backwards

Baa beating sheep
And I opened an eye
Beating of the counting of sheep

Others baa back sheep
And Bo keeps an eye
Of the discipline of kinds of sheep

GUARDIAN

Contrast Rooster's white feathers
With the greater surrounding darkness,
But he sings with all his blue might;
An iconoclast of old scoffs at the ghosts of the pastures,
Bespeaks of himself, stalks and struts in the eerie morning moonlight;
But he sings with all his white might,
Because truthfully he is our gentleman of the darkness,
And out in Bo Peeps' pasture land, and morning miles away,
He is the savior. He is the guardian of the new dawn.

WHITE MICE

Somewhere in back of the stars,
But the white mice invading the moon tonight
    Must have come from the Milky Way

TOADSTOOL

I don't know why I pursed my lips
That can have told the story of a ring of gold
I don't know why I swallowed a blacksnake once
Yet at the bottom of my heart that is being a toadstool
I don't know why I clung to a dark railing once
And wanted the eel for the dark railing
To have crawled to the mouth of the gold ringer
I don't know why I held an eel at arm's length
And wanted its sinewy muscles to have crawled to a toad's strength
I don't know why the sea is boiling hot
That I looked over the dark railing
I don't know why I wanted a salt pond that is muddier
To have been full of thingamajigs that clung to snails
And asked more seaweed questions, and different kinds of things

WELLS

What do you know of others
What do you know of their dreams
What do you know of water on the desert
What do you know of water everywhere
What do you know of a cloud in the sky
What do you know of the three rivers that run deeper
What do you know of the three rivers that have cast their shadows
    above ground
What do you know of those wandering eyes

WONDERLAND

Nevertheless, Alice, Plymouth Rock
Was never to be of glass and sand and sea;
Moreover those had been English glass stepping stones
Up onto the House of Lords through the Looking Glass;
That had been a land of glass and sand and steeples;
They'd left England; they'd left a glass Wonderland

BAYTOWN

But do you know a martyr
That has been stoned at stonehaven?
Do you know of a stone lion
That guarded the stone harbor?
Do you know of a peaceful vessel that sunk in the bay?
Do you know of the quiet news through the bay town?
Do you know of long ago?
Do you know of the hands of a sea lion?
That has added centuries of sand
And left some drouth on the mouth of the sea lion

WORDS ENDS

If a man walketh within a city
Is he shaped of that city around
The waistline of the river's end

If a man talketh within a city
Shaped his words of that city around
The tongue line of the river's bend

For if a man thinketh within a city
Draped his thoughts of that city around
There is soot and smoke above the river's bend

Of his thoughts of the down of a thistle
And leaves his talk tongued around
The mainline between the city's end

For if a man screameth within a city
Sire shaped of the city, around
The noon whistles at the head of the bend

His dreams are of time and a whistle
His talk is smoky fast shaped around
The tongue line of the hired city's bend

And he is the talk of the city
And he is the shape of that city
And what are his words of that city, around
And around the great city's bends

FOOLSCAP BAY

I wondered if it wasn't a fierce clown with a crosswhip
that rode through its veins last night
the night was cold and dark and blustery
the wind in its foolscap ruffled the night skies
the dark clouds touched the moon
the wind rattled the windows again with all its might
there were some all clear signals so on through the night
and all was so safe and sound

THE LITTLE SHOP AROUND THE CORNER

the moon was as hard as the cupboard was bare
the moon was as hard as the land I ever lived on
the moon was as hard as the pavements
the moon was as hard as a stonewall I ever slept on
the moon was as hard as the sidewalks of heaven
the moon was as hard as where the roads led to
the moon was as hard as where the sidewalks led to
the moon was as hard as the little shop around the corner
the moon was as hard as a dime I found on the moon

FOR MAIN ST.

now, if you took all of Main St. as long as it is
all over the world, and took all of that lone way of being,
less understandably, and wound it around the moon,
for a banker has escaped from a farmer
for a banker has been collecting more of our stars

DARK FLOWERS

Know of a stonewall that has windows?
Know of pulling the shades down?
Know of a stonewall for dividing our lives from the lives of
    the poor?
Know of cement leaves?
Know of the flowers that have puzzled ourselves all of our
    lives long?

TWIN LAKES

In a land of silver bells, of silver deer, of silver ears
Of lakefulness lest there be awakefulness
Morning shivers silver before their ears
Not a sound shivers before their lakefulness
Of awakefulness of doubly morning deer

Trancelike, silently, if ever a silver rustle,
But not a sound creeps before their ears,
Though one lake morning star sees of them
In a land of heavenly lakefulness
Of awakefulness of doubly morning deer

FIREFLIES

that lifted their elbows
on top of the eyesockets
that blinded the sunshine
in the presence of everyone
that lifted the fiery tales
there are that are to be told
out of the night

those are the fiery angels there are
tomorrow that summed up the sunsets
those are the morning angels there are
yesterday that drifted over the dawns
and wanted more stars during the night
are they the little peoples of unrest?
that lived for a day and a night
that accounted for the morning stars
that live with the moon sunsets

EVENING

Our world was nearer by
Even our hearts beat stronger
Even the squirrels ran thicker in the evening dusk
Even the chickens caught their feathers where we were and stayed
Of the sound of an approaching evening angel
    Another evening ran to the edge of the world

SUMMER ANGEL

that I do know
that art is a séance that created the rose

that I do know
that art is a séance between you and I and the rose

that I do know
of time and space and a pastime summer angel

that I do know
that art is the dream that came to be the rose

OUT OF THE INKWELL

but I wanted the moon
to have dwindled down to the size of the golden inkwell
in the daylight tonight
for I wanted to have told the story of our stars

FOR A RUSTY GATE

What do you know
Of a note of reason?

What do you do
With a pencil
For a rusty gate?

for if you'll think this over
       for sound and hammer and reasonableness
for an iron typewriter that doesn't lift a key today
       wasn't to have been used since yesterday

THEY ARE THE SCARLET BIRDS

Why, they are the birds
That wanted to come to life and sing again
That only the poets knew of

Why, they were the scarlet birds that everyone said
Were too scarlet ever to be remembered again

Why, these are the places to be remembered,
And whenever these birds are to be remembered again,
Singing

Why, they are the scarlet birds and the bright flowers
No longer with us

But these are the empty places remembered
And shall be no more birds singing

But they'll sing in your hearts, poets,
They'll sing ever again

They are the scarlet birds, and the bright flowers,
That ever came to be, and to sing again

HAPPILY

Of an architectural squirrel
That keeps silver keys for silver locks
And treasure their walnuts for them

THANKSGIVING

Are you a cold Thanksgiving flower?
Did you put the flower in the vase?
Were you in the garden the day before yesterday
Before the pilgrims came and took your things away?
Did you cut the turkey alone?
Why this isn't to be of the servility of a slave?
Are you a cold nymph of November?
That you'd put the flower in the vase

WILHELM'S

Aw, why didn't you say pie and cake?
And pie in the sky
And a nickel in the slot, and to boot,
And that's all I had
At the bottom of my heart
That I needed another dime, and to boot;
Aw, why didn't you say half witted?,
And wanted the feathers put back on the owl, to loot,
That old Father Wilhelm had ordered a lot
And had turkey and pie and a heart,
An owl for a nickel shot out of the whole slot

BRONZE

Why, I know of a bronze lock and key
That was to be kept, and kept securely,
  And locked to the bronze sunsets

Why, I know of a bronze day in December
That I'd stayed by a bronze window shade indefinitely
  And locked the cold dream to my breast

Why, I remember a bronze thermometer at noon
That locked the sunrises and the sunsets
  At a December reading that stayed dim and cold

Why, I remember securely a bronze evening
That I'd stayed by a lamp, and kept memorabilia of the sunsets
  And locked the noon and the moon and the cold stars

PAST MEMPHIS

Finally that isn't a showboat at all
that doesn't have bales and bales of August
cotton to show for itself

that'll be some music on board
for the Captain during September
but more of these boats for thryme
are on their way up north to give
their thread to a higher landowner

SHEEP

Even the sheep's woolen
Clung in the June distance
And I wanted the needle
That passed through the sheep's woolen
To have caught onto a thread
To a cloud that stayed in the sky

TENEMENT

What do you know of sundown?
What do you know of our New Jersey iron saints?
What an ugly bunny!
What an ugly blotch!
Westside New Yorkers are at their windowpanes
The N.J. bunny is a visitor
The sun is hoarse visiting their windowpanes

Another evening is quieter
The sun isn't so uproarious
Jersey City is abounding in these lights
What are the inhabitants?
What names of old!
Ghirlandaio, Fra Lippi, and Montagna's grocery store,
The name of Leonardo DaVinci appears at a letter box at a doorway,
The green Madonna is on the lawn in some little park nearer by,
What a pageant this is just before dark
Only the poor know of such things
Only the poor know of this nativity
The sun that is red floods the pavements and the sidewalks
The sun creeps along these tenement vines
The sun visits these windowpanes this evening
The sun that is red falls on the floor
This is the night of our dear saviour's birth

AUGUST DRAGONFLY

even an August dragonfly
    first recedes backwards
when that is the summer dragonfly needle
        that plunges the thread forwards

PASTURE LANDS AWAY

There are dreams, some are dreams,
And there are dreams of colors,
Of rainbows out in Bo Peep's pasture lands,
Some of these are dreams I never meant to come to be,
And out on sunset prairie, Abandonment of dreams,
Some have been dreams of the horseless stagecoach
And further and further and pasture lands away

BEWILDERMENT

For I don't know why
I drew a line to the end of a field
I made that a slender plow
I put all of them up against a summer sky

Nor do I know why
I drew a line from there to one cloud
I made that a bead of sweat
That stayed and strayed against the dark sky

MORESO

Are you whistling
At the back of the dark hallway?
All I do know about dark life
About three rickety flights upstairs.
Are you barked at tonight
By a puppy? that would if he could
Have fed you all the dog biscuits
You wanted, or ever could have—

DEIGN TO DESIGN

If
it's
a
steel pin

It
isn't
to
dig your grave with

If
it's
dug
already

THINK THIS OVER

just before
you left

just before
you shouldered a gun

just before
you left

the thunder
there is in the grass

WHERE RESIDES THE SINEWY LIZARD

At the back of the skull Tonight I knew of the House
That lodged the living muscle that clung to the starlight

CORNUCOPIA

Why time stitched a word for a hornet's nest
That said to the little knives there are
That have been offered for a sword in time
Though for the center of the curious circus
Time said to a duncelike being that is ourselves
Yet fiercely that is an angel of another kind
Time sought along a cornucopia vine divergently
Still time said to the little spheres there are
That have been offered for the agony of time

MAINE

Maybe we found another word in the mist
Maybe we found another cucumber during our garden travels
Maybe we found another word for a bluebird
That flew higher and higher up in the blue sky
Maybe we found another gray cloud somewhere
Where sheep gathered in the prolonged mist
Maybe we were all poets today and tomorrow
Maybe we found another word for a bluebird
That flew over a gray cloud in the distance

GUEST OF THE MONTH OF MAINE

That I shall have been a hunted fire in the Wilderness!,
That I have leapt at the frenzied pines
And chased the squirrels from their haunts and habits; –
Shall have leapt at the forest bookshelves,
And shall have kept their forest walnuts for me
At the Top of a House of flames!
Shall have cut off their tails with the carving knife,
And fire and sword!
And afterwards, and ever afterwards,
And kept the freedom of the wilderness to Myself;
Yet I am a friend of the winds that have leapt with me at the pines
Oh Wild, but I have denied the freedom of the wilds,
Oh, burning bright!, but I am the kingdom of fire and sword.
Oh Wild, Myself!, I am hunted, I am lost,
In the Wilderness I am a king without a queen,
I have kept my spear of lightning to the Top of the House!
Shall I have been invited like a shadow to the forest and the wild
Yet I have caught on fire!
That I shall have been a king of fire and armour
During my own kinds of devastation,
And leapt at the frenzied freedom of the wilds!

RISING SUN

Still that is the rising sun
That sung to the black beetle in its hideout,
Where there shall be light,
But interlacing light there shall be darkness
And the black beetle that knew of the song
Of the rising star for the sunshine
    Burrowed deeper into the surrounding darkness

SPRING LAKE

Ironically, thank your iron stars, bub
Ever to think a link, to have linked seaweed, bub
At length, At strength – for lock and key,
Oh, how hard! Oh how hard at the bottom of the Lake,
I have survived an iron sea bubble, for a cushion,
To have peeped through a keyhole at salt and spray and silver stars

EVENTFUL ANGELS

We lived under a dark moon
How a chain is being wound
through our lives
That counted the seconds eerily
during time

We lived during darkness
We shall have been further enchanted
during a chain of events
That added our lives differently
during time

We lit a candlelight on another star
We explored another kind of darkness
during our lives
We explored other kinds of angels
during time

We lived during an enchanted forest
We re-discovered our own star
during a trail of events
That reasoned our lives differently
during time

But we lived during a wilderness
That mysteriously wound the chimes
through our lives
That counted the eventful angels
during time

HOLD FAST, ARMY BUTTONS

Ironically, those are brass buttons
that are made of holdfast iron

Dumbfounded, those are brass knuckles
to have been tied to just straightjackets

Those are a tyrant's muscles
to your best vest buttons

17, LIFE ON A DESTROYER

simply isn't like paddling a canoe,
    finally I wanted to have paddled my own canoe

and Indians who had been Indians told me their stories,
    about wherever it was I could have paddled my own canoe,

simply isn't like building a straw in the winds,
    to wherever it was I could have paddled my own canoe,

simply isn't like building anything at all out of a paddle
    about wherever it was I could have lifted a straw over a paddle,

simply isn't building a leanto out of a paddle,
    about wherever it was I could have paddled my books to a leanto,

and fiddled, and paddled my own canoe tomorrow,
    about wherever it was I could have built anything out of
        anything at all

SEDGELING

I am spent upon the rocks, sedgeling
My days are spent upon the coastline
Upon the rocky shoulder of Maine
I am lashed inwards by salt and wind and spray
Seagulls fly to seagulls in mid air
I am entranced, I am enchanted,
Alone, the sea is spent upon the coastline
The war of the sea rises and falls amongst the rocky shoulders
I'll wander further, sedgeling,
I'll stand to greet the seagulls that cry in the mist
Wander in and amongst the boulders that have broken the strife pin
I'll find the bloody answer, sedgeling,
Somewhere upon the rocky shoulder of Maine

INCHES

I wondered if we weren't lonely for the golden dark smiles
That returned to us during the month of September causes

I wondered if their enslavement to a dark ruler
That counted the inches of their lives together

I wondered if we weren't orphans
Who returned those smiles to others

I wondered what those golden dark smiles said to one another

I wondered of the gold on the moon
I wondered of the golden key I held in my hand
That unlocked the moon for ourselves

I wondered of our freedoms
We'd rather have been orphans

PEACE—1934-1939

Gosh, it didn't last very Long
   It was a proud gray deserted Feeling,
Come comfortable out of a Fog—
      To boot or to bootless and onto dry Martinis
    Until finally a dark brown taste
                 Set down in the back of its Mouth,
    Fog drifting away—we had to know what it was—
    Being driven by war monsters

THAT WROTE ON THE BACK OF THE BOX

of the phantasmagoria of a sedge match
that wrote on the back of the box

quickly!

that said, I love you, hello

PRISONERS

Steel silence hangs in the balance
That those are a man's dimelike thoughts

Though, send us a bar of gold
Send us a bar of heavenly morning chanter
Send us a note of the sun's dust
That rings in a prisoner's hands

Send us the sun's late afternoon lamp
That hangs golden on the floor
That breaks the silence of the steel links

For the silence of our enchanted laughter to ourselves
Is painful to the steel bars that stay in the balance

Though send us a note of the sun's dust
That laughed heartily in a prisoner's hands

Send us reading material, for the sun,
That lightened the particles of black gold

Send us smiles
Send us golden dark smiles

ANTE, 1910

Why, the dawn is in the mountains,
But the sun was to have been speared by an Indian tonight
And rolled westward, and rolled onwards;
But the sun is an Ante,
But the sun is for an old sedge hammer
That rolled out of the eastern ranges, pacifically,
But the sun will be a buffalo on the western waters tonight,
Specifically, for an old sedge hammer that struck downwards,
But the sun is for a nickel's worth of chimes

JUNE SILVER

I wanted you to know of
The black June bug
That buzzed silver

But I wanted you to know of
June silver, of blue silver
During the month of June

I wanted you to know
I rocked in a rocking chair
And all along the silvery vines

I wanted you to know I knew
Of a boy who rocked on top of a rocking horse
And up and down the wiry plains

I wanted you to know of
Blue silver, of black silver
During the month of June silver

Selections from Hamilton's final notebooks

MIRRORLAND

I wanted to know more of the soldiers
On the other side of the looking glass
I wanted to know how they got there
What they are doing there
I wanted to know more of myself around them
How I got there
Why I got there
What I am doing there again
I wanted to know more of memories
I wanted to know more of remembrances
I wanted to know more of myself
On the other side of the looking glass

THE WAR OF THE ROSES

I thought of the rose and its thorns
I thought of the rose and its sorrow
I thought of the war of the roses
I thought of the boy and the girl and his shadow
I thought of Alice
I thought of Alice as other than Alice in Wonderland
I thought of love's sweet surrender
I thought Alex surrendered his soul to Alice
I thought of the soul

MIRRORLAND

I thought of the other side of the looking glass
I thought of Alice as other than Alice in Wonderland
I thought it risked its truth
I thought it risked fairyland
I thought it risked light years
I thought Alice risked her long curls
I thought Alice lived differently
I thought Alice did what Alice did
I thought Alice lived for the soul

VIRGINIA BEACH

I think of the tug of the tides
I think of the tug of the tides on the shoreline
I think of the tug of the tides on Virginia Beach
I think it tugs at the pearly gates
I think it tugs on the seaweed
I think it explains a little boy's hair
I think it explains a little boy's tears
I think it explains a little boy's whereabouts
I think it explains the soul

GLAD TIDINGS

I think there is a mermaid in the water
I think it tugs on the pulse
I think it tugs on the pulsations
I think it sings in the azure
I think it sings in the breezes
I think it sings in the branches
I think it sings in the trees
I think it sings in the leaves
I think it sings in the seaweed
I think it sings in the sky above
I think it sings rockaby baby in the treetop
I think it sings for a fair day
I think it sings for a boy who is going to go to the fairy world
I think it sings of the poet laureate
I think it sings for a boy who is going to wear long hair
I think it sings glad tidings
I think it sings of the soul

STARS

I know of the stars on the back of a butterfly
I know of the stars there are in the universe
I know of paradise
I know of fairyland
I know of the dreams
I know of the soul

*Title illegible

I think of the sunlight peeping through our windows
I think of the sunlight peeping through the N.H. countryside
I think the colonel is amazed
I think we are all amazed
I think Hiawatha is doing his long hair this morning
I think of touching one of these beautiful N.H. lakes
I think of first touching sunlight
I think of first touching a cloud
I think of first touching the soul

THE CAINE MUTINY

I am around
I am around differently
I am around a woman who is showing them herself
I thought of showing them myself
I thought it needed to be admired
I thought it needed to be admired differently
I thought I admired myself
I thought I did my long hair in bows
I thought I admired my long hair
I thought I explained my whereabouts
I thought I explained my full soul
I thought I explained my full adventure

SUNDOWN

I thought of the pacific
I thought of the island in the sunset hours
I thought of the golden bees that sing in the evening sunshine
(I thought of the golden bees that sing in the sunshine out west)
I thought of the golden bees that sing in a boy's long hair
I thought it can be done
I thought it can be said of the soul

SCHOOLDAYS

I did the schooldays
I did what the girls did
I did the morning sunshine
I did my long hair on Tuesday
I did the hammer on the school bell
I did over the river and through the woods
I did education
I did this with all my thoughts
I did this with all my might
I did my full soul

SHADOWLAND

I think it does this in shadowland
I think it does the sun playing with the clouds
I think it does the boy and the girl and the parlor
I think it does the boy and the girl and a soldier
I think it does love's sweet surrender
I think it does this in fairyland
I think it does the boy surrendering his soul to the girl
I think it does the boy surrendering his soul

SUNBURST

I was urged
I couldn't say no
I didn't say no
It was stronger than myself
I was going to do what girls do
I was going to be a beautiful nurse
I flowed with the sunburst on the classroom window
I tied a ribbon in my long brown hair
I began my life's ambition
I began my soul

FREE

I dared
I dared to go further
I dared to go fuller
I dared to go everywhere
I dared the four winds
I dared to do what the girls do
I dared to wear my long hair all over the place
I dared joy
I dared happiness
I dared to be free
I dared my own soul

Acknowledgements

Along with the poems that have been collected here for the first time, *A Dark Dreambox of Another Kind* includes many poems that had previously been published in *The Poems of Alfred Starr Hamilton* (The Jargon Society, 1970), and in the chapbooks *Sphinx* (Kumquat Press, 1969) and *The Big Parade* (The Best Cellar Press, University of Nebraska, 1982).

Thanks to the poetry archives and archivists at the University of Buffalo, who allowed us access to their extensive collection of journals and manuscripts and to Jonathan Williams's papers, where many unpublished poems were found. Thanks also to The University of Chicago for allowing us access to David Ray's papers in their Special Collections Research Center, where we were able to read more unpublished work of Hamilton's, along with pages and pages of Hamilton and Ray's intimate correspondence.

We'd also like to thank Virginia Cruickshank, Jane Huber, David and Kathie Cruickshank, and the rest of Alfred's family, as well as Michael Basinski, Peter Gizzi, Geof Hewitt, Thomas Meyer, George and Diana Moser, Geoffrey G. O'Brien, Michael Silverblatt, Trevor Winkfield, and especially Charles North – for his guidance and his cosmic ability to be at the right place at the right time. Lastly, thanks to the publishers of *Adventures in Poetry*, *Cat's Eye*, *Exquisite Corpse*, *Fire Exit*, *Monks Pond*, *Lips*, *New Directions*, *New Letters*, *Wormwood Review*, and *Epoch*, where some of these poems first appeared.